COACHING
CONVERSATIONS
THAT COUNT

COACHING
CONVERSATIONS
THAT COUNT

Leading Teams with Continuous Conversations

EMILY NIGHTINGALE

this Book

ISBN 978-0-9991198-4-6
E-book ISBN 978-0-9991198-5-3

For further information, please contact the author at emily@emilynightingaleauthor.com

Or visit:
www.emilynightingaleauthor.com.

Hundred Acre Press LLC
P.O. Box 54316
Cincinnati, OH 45254

http://www.hundredacrepress.com

Contents

COACHING
CONVERSATIONS
THAT COUNT

Everyone Loves Stan

EVERYONE LOVES STAN... his team, his family, and everyone in upper management at his company all think he is a great guy, a great manager, friend, spouse, dad. How can anyone be loved by all?

Stan is authentic, honest and caring, and he lets people know it. You can be all those things, too, but if it isn't communicated to others, no one really knows you. Stan has made an effort to know his team. He knows what is important to them. He is aware of their individual goals, and what they care about at work and in life. He shares stories with them of his experiences and his family. They know what he cares about and what is important to him. They know how their goals and Stan's goals fit into the vision for the team. They understand where the team fits into the company's vision.

Upper management finds Stan to be model manager. He gets things done. They never hear complaints about him or his team. Stan is easy to work with—he takes direction, but he also questions a directive, when necessary, in a non-confrontational manner.

In order to challenge the members of his team, Stan wants to be sure each person is in the right role, and he needs to be sure that the growth challenges he gives to people are the right ones. He can't do that without understanding their strengths and capabilities. He cares about their successes.

Stan's team members, as well as his friends and family, know they can talk to him about any work issues they have, or even a personal issue, and they trust Stan to support them and to keep their conversations private. Stan earned this trust by the way he communicates with them, and by the alignment of his actions. His integrity shows when he speaks, in the way he speaks, in the content of his words, and the actions he takes.

We all communicate in different ways, but much of the time we communicate through conversation. Facial expressions, body language, and sometimes silence play a role in those conversations. Sometimes conversations go nowhere, and it seems like we are just filling the air with words, even though we think we are getting a point across. Other times, a brief conversation changes us. It can change your path, your attitude, or your view of yourself or someone else. What's the difference? How can we do this purposely? Keep reading, as we talk through many important factors that affect our conversations.

Conversations have different levels and much of the time we communicate on the surface.

How are you today?

Fine. Good. Glad it's Friday.
Ugh, it's Monday.
Can't wait for Fall weather.

How are things going?

Oh, pretty much the same. There
was one issue with the network this
week, and I spoke to Jim and he is
tracking down the issue. There was a
misunderstanding with Jane over whose
responsibility it was to post the news
article, but I took care of it.

I got a 98 on my exam.

These are surface conversations.

> ⊡ *Surface conversations don't change anything. They are emotionless and are essentially filling the air with words or just reporting information that could be transmitted through email.*

Text, email, and social media have changed the habits of communication to a surface level for many of us. Some people refuse to be on social media for this very reason. It expands the number of people in your world, but leaves many of your connections at the surface. Others are known for sharing too much information on social media with people who are not in a close relationship. This makes people uncomfortable. The art of conversation is to have depth in your conversation with those who are comfortable with that depth, and not with those who are not comfortable with it.

Good relationships, in general, are an important ingredient to finding joy in life, and by good, I mean those with depth. It's the deeper relationships that sustain us and help us grow as people.

⊡ *Good work relationships make things go better at work—they may be the source of opportunities, or may sprout the seed of an idea. They also motivate people to develop their skills, work harder, progress in their careers, and hopefully spend more time at the same company.*

Stan understands this. He talks with people face-to-face, and gives them his full attention when he does. He does not look at his phone or let email or other people interrupt conversations. This makes his team members (and family) feel that they are important enough for his attention. He is also punctual to meetings. Being regularly late to meetings and interruptions make people feel they are not important to you. Stan is a good listener, and he is thoughtful about what he says when he speaks.

The Art of Conversation

THE ART OF great conversation is to say the right thing at the right time, and to not only feel understood, but to actually be understood. It takes some skill and personal comfort to take the conversation below the surface level.

This is why great conversation is not found on social media. It is found in person. It is found one-on-one and in groups.

Level 1: Social/Small Talk

Level 1 is the Social level of conversation. This is elevator talk or cafeteria line talk. You can start a conversation with anyone with basic subjects like the weather, or baseball, or the company picnic. If small talk doesn't advance beyond to the

Intellectual/Facts level, you may never really get to know this person. Body language is in play here. Part of the conversation involves eye contact, whether the person is abrupt or friendly, if they seem like they want to talk all day, or if they are trying to get away.

It's easy to step from this level into the next level. An example is the old gentleman I met at the tire store last week. He was waiting to have his car serviced, and I was waiting for an oil change. I was trying to do some work on my laptop, when he started telling me about why he switched from a different car repair shop. I was receptive to listening to him for a few minutes about his car repair woes, and then he asked me if I'd ever been to Nashville. He told me he grew up there, and then started to go on about how much he had loved Hank Williams and the Grand Ole Opry. He was trying to elevate the conversation into Level 2 intellectual/facts disclosure. He was clearly bored while waiting for his car and just wanted to talk for a while. I was polite and talked to him for a few minutes and then went back to work. I didn't encourage him, so the conversation didn't progress.

Level 2: Intellectual/Facts

Level 2 is the intellectual level of conversation, with sharing of facts. A lot of our professional conversations stay at the intellectual level. We can share ideas, plans, strategies and facts with others without really getting to know someone personally. When you share facts about yourself with another person, you start to learn something about who they are, and what you have in common. You may wish to stay at this level, unless you start connecting and finding each other more interesting on a personal level.

Even some marriages never dare to go beyond this level, or if they have at some point, they may decide they need to pull it back to Level 2 in order to convince themselves they are happy enough to stay married.

After 20 years of marriage, my husband gave me two Linda Ronstadt CDs for a Christmas gift. Seeing the puzzled look on my face, he said, "You used to play her songs all the time." I said, "Yes, I remember twenty years ago when I did. Thank you." I never played the CDs. No offense to Linda, but I hadn't listened to any of her music for 20 years. The year before that he gave me a keyboard I didn't know how to play. I was stunned at the realization that after 20 years of being together, he didn't seem to know enough about me to buy me a gift. I think that we must have stepped back to Level 2 in our relationship many years earlier. Those two gifts and that single conversation made me realize he didn't really know me for all those years.

> ▣ *You may discover that you have to stay at Level 2 conversations in order to stay in your job, or in your marriage, or sometimes to maintain a relationship with one of your siblings or parents. It can keep the relationship where it is now, when you are afraid of how things might change if emotions or opinions are involved.*

People have different viewpoints on how much they share with co-workers and managers about themselves. You may not have things in common with them other than the work, or for the level of trust needed to step into Level 3 conversations at work, or sometimes at home. But Level 3 is where the conversation magic lies. The real connections begin in Level 3. However, both parties need to feel safe enough to enter Level 3 conversations.

Level 3: Emotional/Opinions

Level 3 is where emotions and opinions enter the conversation. After connecting socially and then intellectually, do I feel comfortable sharing my opinions with this person? Opinions have emotional attachments, and some opinions shouldn't be shared at work. Religion and politics are subjects that can get very heated emotionally, which is why people avoid these subjects at work and often stay at the Intellectual conversation level. This conversation level usually elevates when you want to wade into a more personal connection with someone.

Often people want emotional connections badly, but don't know how to make them happen. This is the level that changes us, and I think we know that unconsciously, which is why we long for it. It can change how we see ourselves, change our paths in life, and change our attitudes in a single conversation. Often we don't get to this level because we feel vulnerable, or don't think the other person has any interest in hearing about our feelings, dreams, passions, or anything else that is personal. Level 3 requires a deeper level of trust in another person to treat our conversations with respect, and not to hurt or reject us. Change and development only happen when conversations can get to this level. If you want to have this connection with someone, you can invite them by asking a question, or you can share something about yourself and see how they respond.

Level 4: Spiritual

The next level is Spiritual conversation. This is reserved for really close connections. I would say I have this connection with my children and they have this with each other. They can be hundreds of miles away from each other and know when something is wrong. Sometimes you just know when someone close to you needs your support. These are people you trust with your authentic self. At this level, you can say exactly what is on your mind without worrying about the response of the other person, as this person knows you well and accepts how you think. Conversations are very open-natured. A simple look or a few words can tell the other person exactly what you are thinking because you share this level of conversational connection.

> ▣ *A single conversation (or gift)*
> *can change your direction, or*
> *trigger a decision, so it's crucial*
> *to be purposeful about them*
> *and to know which level you*
> *are experiencing.*

I remember a time when a single conversation changed my direction. At a company where I worked, I was pondering applying for a different job in a different division of the company. I had been in the same job for seven years, and my department had recently gone through some changes and we had a new VP. I had stalled on applying for the job and was talking myself out of taking the leap. There were probably two sentences uttered by the VP about his plans for our department, in a single, short conversation, that sent me racing down to HR to see if I could still apply for the other job. I didn't even stop at my desk. I don't even remember what he said, but I remember how it made me feel. A single conversation could also reverse someone's decision to leave.

Now that we have covered the levels of conversation, you can refer back to these when thinking about specific people in your life. What level of conversations are you having with them? Let's chart them out.

You can use a grid like the one below for this.

Name/Level

____

____

____

____

____

Why Continuous Conversations?

CONTINUOUS CONVERSATIONS ARE crucial to the development of relationships and individuals via interaction. You can't wait until your kid is leaving for college to prepare him to make good decisions. You start preparing him with every conversation from the minute he was put in your arms at the hospital as an infant (or the backseat of the taxi, depending on your circumstances.) Children learn what kind of support and feedback to expect from you. They learn what you think when they make wrong choices, and how you react when they make their mistakes as they are growing up. This is how they learn boundaries. You learn who they are and what they need from you, and also what they don't need from you. You support them by helping them understand better choices as they are learning from their mistakes.

I noticed at around age 10, my eldest daughter seemed to have no opinion about a lot of things. She would just let me decide things for her, which makes it easy for me, but at some point I worried that she would let other people make decisions for her when she was out in the world. So I started asking her opinion about everything. What should we have for dinner? What color should I paint this room? What should we do today? Do you like these curtains, or are these better? I forced her to make decisions. I could imagine her telling her friends that her mom couldn't make decisions on her own. "She always asks me what to do." I wanted her to practice, practice, practice making decisions to help her develop confidence. This required me to continually find ways to include her on decisions.

You wouldn't meet with your child every March to tell him or her what is good and bad about what he or she did over the year, the way traditional performance reviews are done. You correct or praise your kids in the moment. They get an A on a test and you praise them. There is no "but"—"It's great that you got an A but you didn't take out the trash last night." You just praise them for the A. He didn't take out the trash, though, so at the appropriate time, you call him out for that. You don't combine these or save them up for the end of the month or the end of the year.

The same concept holds true with your dog. If your dog pees on the floor or runs out in the street in front of a car, you don't correct the behavior the next week or month, or year. If you care anything about her, you do it right away.

> "Petunia, last November you ran
> out in front of a car. Stop doing that.
> You'll get killed!"

See, this doesn't make any sense at all. By the same token, you want to reinforce good behavior and you do it right away:

> "Stay, Petunia. Good girl!
> Here is a treat for you."

The longer someone does something the wrong way, the more it is instilled as a habit, and the more difficult it is to change it.

Now for a chance to get on my soapbox. At my children's elementary school, they were experimenting with something called "inventive spelling" to encourage kids to write more, prior to having learned to spell correctly. They wouldn't correct the spelling of certain words until certain grades. So, for example, they let them spell a word wrong until fourth grade, when this word appeared on a list for fourth graders, and it was now expected to be spelled correctly. I hated this process. You can't let kids spell a word wrong for four years, and then start correcting it. I'm still annoyed about this. They derailed the process of learning to spell correctly for hundreds of children. This process never made sense to me.

> ⊡ *With your family, friends and work team, continuous conversations are the only way to promote good habits, efficiency, and continuous positive development.*

I would resent someone for letting me do something wrong and waiting until a performance review to tell me about it . . . maybe enough to look for another job.

If you are managing a team or a family, don't let your focus on results become so narrow that you are overlooking caring about the people part of the equation. There are deadlines and goals and plenty of things that have to be done, but continuous building of relationships and connections with everyone are part of that process. Don't feel you can skip this and just use pressure or power to guide people to action. It may save time on a certain day by skipping a discussion, but it does not build a culture of engagement and development of people, which is in the purview of being a manager. You'll waste more time training replacements as people flee from your team (unless we're talking about family members and then you'll have to do all the chores yourself.)

In sales training, they say that customers want to buy from people they like. They also want to work for people they like. They also say people leave their managers, not companies. Don't let your perception of yourself blind you to the way you connect with others. Try to get some feedback, although it sometimes isn't easy. People get trained to give you the kind of feedback you subtly let them know you want. (She only wants positive feedback / He only wants us to agree with him.) You'll have to try hard to find ways to get the real feedback.

And you need to give real feedback, just as you would give your dog when she runs out in the street. If you care about the people in your life, and their development, you'll find the guts to give them real feedback. If you are recognizing and praising the great things they do at other times, and have developed a relationship of trust and integrity, they'll appreciate constructive feedback from you, because it's balanced with the positive. They know you are aware of their accomplishments, too.

In your approach to each person as an individual, consider what you know about them. In a work situation and at home, people think differently about how adaptable they are to change. This has to be considered when you are trying to understand how people think. You have the early-adopters, the visionaries, who leap onto new ideas and are ready to push an idea down the road—maybe without fully vetting it. They may be extremely open to new thoughts and opinions, but they will push back if you are trying to slow them down with checks and balances.

You have the conservative folks, who are comfortable with all the current processes and are reluctant to change them, maybe because they know the history of why you do things the way you do. Or they don't want change just because they understand the process, and it makes sense to them. They may fear new ideas because they don't fully understand the effect an idea will have on what they do, or if their services will still be required. How will they respond? They may push you back if you are trying to push them forward.

Then you have the ones in the middle, who will go along with either one, if it makes sense.

They might be waiting for someone else to make a decision or test the waters. They may be more receptive to what you have to say than the other two groups.

Knowing more about each person can help you understand where they fall in their willingness to take on new things and move forward. This helps you gauge what kinds of challenges and opportunities will work for them.

As more people work remotely, it may take more purposeful effort to connect with people when you are in the office, or by instant message, text or phone. This continuous connection lets people know that you think about them and value them. If a week goes by, and you have not connected in some way with a person on your team, or in your immediate world, that is a long time. I know you're busy—we all are. That doesn't change anything.

Connecting via Mindset

BEFORE YOU CAN have a fruitful conversation with another person, you have to know yourself. What are some of the things you know about yourself that have interfered with candid conversation with others? Self-awareness is an important ingredient in coaching.

Make a list of a few things here (no one is perfect)

____

____

____

____

The brain works in very interesting ways that we don't completely understand, especially in relationships. We get signals from our brains whether to trust from one area:

Pre-frontal cortex:
Is this person credible?

and distrust from another area:

Amygdala:
Should I run for it?

These signals may occur in your brain from an encounter with another person sometimes before you even have a conversation with them, and you may not understand why it is happening. We often respond automatically to someone's words or actions, or even their presence, without consciously understanding why we are doing it.

Trust and distrust are in two separate parts of your brain. You may trust what someone is saying, while another part of your brain is telling you not to trust this person. The distrust signal might occur first. If distrust occurs, the amygdala sends an alert signal to the pre-frontal cortex. There isn't a lot you can do about this, other than to make an effort to instill trust, and to make sure you know yourself before embarking on coaching someone else. Identify any communication issues **you** have, so that you can be aware when you are getting a response that isn't what you expected. When you are consciously aware of how you come across in conversations, or any misunderstandings you have had in the past, you can handle any similar misunderstandings in the moment.

Tom said that what gets in the way of trust in conversation with his manager is knowing that his manager always represents the enterprise, and is always doing what upper management wants, even if it isn't in his best interest. If his manager had some flexibility in how she ran the department and was transparent with him, Tom thinks that it would make it easier to have candid conversations. It also sounds like there may be some misalignment with Tom goals and the company's goals. It would be important for his manager to develop good conversational skills to work out any misunderstandings with Tom, and not lose a good employee.

Nancy, who manages a team of project managers, said that she tries to have as much transparency as possible with her team. She is upfront about it when there is something she can't share, but they know she is willing to share as much information as she can with them. Nancy works on her ability to have uncomfortable conversations with individuals on her team, when necessary.

Being a manager isn't all sunshine and roses. Nancy said it isn't easy sometimes, but rather than avoiding conversations, she works at how to improve her skills in this area. She has seen a difference in how people respond to her in one-on-one conversations since she has been working on improving her conversational skills. She said it would be easy sometimes to revert to her previous style of avoidance, but she knows how important it is to each member of her team to have a manager that cares about them and is willing to tackle issues together.

Identify
Conversational Clues

ENGAGEMENT IN WORK, and engagement in life is maintained through continuous conversations. The topics and words contain the clues as to what is going in a person's mind and in his or her daily life.

One thing I've noticed over the years is that if something is bothering a person, they will keep bringing up the subject in some way. For example, when a person goes through a breakup of a relationship, they might talk about different memories about that relationship, as they try to trace back (consciously or unconsciously) to see what went wrong and what was good about it. When they have completed that internal process, they will stop talking about it and move on. The clues are in the conversation as to where they are in the process.

There is no blueprint for conversation that works for everyone. We are all individuals with different strengths, different passions, and different lives. That's kind of the point of this book. Guidelines can work well, but you'll need to individualize the guidelines to fit what you know about each person. If you are having continuous conversations, and creating a caring relationship with others, you'll be able to tailor your guidelines to fit the progress and needs of each person. Everyone deserves to get their needs met.

Generational Mindset

PEOPLE GENERALLY SEEM to think Millennials are the only people to want feedback and opportunities for development. I hear this all the time and this is just not true. Many (and to be fair, not all) Millennials were raised a bit differently by parents who gave them more feedback and were more supportive about providing opportunities, so many in this generation have learned to expect that. Baby Boomers and Generation X folks were not raised to expect this, even though they also want the same thing just as much. I think the Baby Boomers who raised the Millennials this way did so because they felt it was something that was missing for them and wanted to make sure their kids had it. They also want it.

It's a matter of expectations—the older generations learned to accept the way things were because it was their reality, especially at work. Younger generations **expect** more feedback and opportunities. All generations **want** it.

> ⊡ *Don't overlook any of the generations in the workplace or at home, as we all want the same thing. Again, everyone deserves to get their needs met.*

Path Mindset

IN YOUR APPROACH to conversation, what do you know about this person? Ignore the generational approach and ask yourself these questions:

- ☐ Is this a go-getter full of ideas and on the fast track to move forward with efficiencies and innovation?

- ☐ Is the person interested in a promotion and have they asked you how to get promoted to management yet?

- ☐ Is this person methodical, detail oriented, and happy doing production type work that never changes?

- ☐ Is this someone that just likes to plan and schedule things in a support role?

☐ Or is this a people person, who enjoys interacting with other people, not computers?

☐ Is this someone who likes to teach and mentor other people?

Strength Mindset

THINK ABOUT THE person's strengths. It may be helpful to have employees take a strengths quiz, or even to write down the top few strengths that you have observed about them. If they are your children or family, you should be able to identify their strengths more easily than someone at work.

It is easier and more feasible to improve strengths than it is to change weaknesses into strengths. If a weakness is preventing someone do his or her job, then by all means, some development work is needed. But for development purposes, maximizing strengths is the best use of effort.

When people have the opportunity to focus on their strengths each day, they are much more engaged in their work, and happier with their lives in general. If you spend your conversations and effort looking for ways to build on people's strengths, your effort will be much more likely to get results. Engagement in work and life comes from pursuing your passions and maximizing your strengths. It helps to have role clarity and to ensure the folks around you are in the correct roles to utilize and enhance their strengths.

One colleague can help another by pointing out a strength of a co-worker. People aren't always aware of those strengths.

⊡ *Often we assume anyone can do the things we find we are good at doing, until someone has a conversation with us and says, "Hey, you are good at that. I struggle with it."*

My son is very talented in working with clay, and still doesn't realize it. He submitted a bust of Shakespeare he made in just a few days for an English class project in high school that was amazing. I'm sure he was looking for the easiest and least painful way to get the project done, without realizing that his work was amazing. His teacher loved it so much she offered to buy it from him to give as a gift to her husband. Over the years, he continues to pursue other areas of interest, but keeps finding himself circling back to working with clay. I still don't think he understands his talent, even though I tell him all the time. I think it's because it comes easily to him and he enjoys it, so he doesn't quite understand the value of what he can do with it. People need feedback from others to help them identify strengths.

Consider someone like Sandy, who joined a team as an admin because she is interested in learning more about what that team does, and how to grow in that area. (Not all team or department admins want that, but if you get to know people, you will find this out about this person.) Sandy is good at being an admin, but she has strengths and passion around the team's purpose, and you could find ways to put that her talents to use while helping her grow in her areas of strength.

If you want to <u>disengage</u> someone from their work, give them a role that doesn't fit, don't connect with them, keep your conversations at Level 1, don't follow through on what you say, and don't provide opportunities to maximize their strengths.

It may sound like a high expectation to do all these things correctly to help engage people with their work, but it isn't too high if you want a high-performing team like Stan's work team. Stan doesn't mind paying attention to all these things, because he understands the importance and contribution of each person on his team. He is also trying to be the best manager he is capable of becoming, so he strives to be a servant leader. He maintains awareness on a daily basis of how he interacts with people and what he needs to do to support them. He doesn't just manage up, but manages across, as well.

Stan is committed to the personal and professional growth of everyone on his team. He thinks beyond the day-to-day realities and learns from the past in order to have the foresight he needs for future plans and decisions.

Feedback as Conversation

HAVING AN OPEN conversation with a person that reports to you is more likely to happen if you can demonstrate that you are also open to feedback from them. If you can get someone to give you feedback, and announce the feedback to the team and let everyone know you are working on it, people might think they could be open to feedback from you. Tell them about the improvement on which you are focused, and ask them to let you know of any occasions where you would be open to a reminder, if by chance, you were not doing what you stated you would do. This is a constructive avenue for opening the conversation door . . . if they think you really mean it. You will know if someone actually reminds you. And your reaction to that reminder is important. Make sure to thank them if they do. Smile and try not to have a "deer in the headlights" look on your face.

When you receive any kind of feedback or ideas during your conversations, remember to always use "Yes and . . ." or "Yes and what else . . ." Never say, "Yes, but . . ." That is like slamming the door in the person's face. "Yes and" is commonly used in improv as a way to extend improvised conversation. You can't improv with a closed door.

Example

Yes but . . . shuts down:

> I think this . . .
> > **Yes, but** we never did because . . .
> Oh, that's right.
> [end of conversation]

Yes and . . . paves the way:

> I think this . . .
> > **Yes, and** we also should this . . .
> > **Yes, and** we could also this . . .
> [and so on]

Yes, and . . . or Yes and what else . . . is a good practice to adopt for you and your team. It opens the door to ideas that can be built by a team by adding and adding and adding to the original suggestion. The person who says "Yes, but . . ." may not realize they are shutting down the other person. They may think they are helping, yet getting a negative vibe from others. This can be confusing and they may not know what to do about it. This simple expression can fix that issue.

I was talking to a mentee about this and I could almost literally see a light bulb go on in his head. His face lit up. He was so excited to learn why his helpfulness wasn't appreciated. He couldn't wait to start using "Yes, and."

He had been struggling in conversations where he was trying to help, and people seemed put off by his efforts. He couldn't figure out why. He immediately realized his "Yes, but" attempts to help were shutting down the conversation instead of helping expand ideas.

When giving and receiving feedback, remember to focus on the situation or behavior. Feedback is taken personally, and you need to do your best to minimize the personal nature of it to make it accepted more easily. Summarize the point you are making and make it brief. Do not go on and on. Follow it with an "I" statement to identify how it made you feel, or state what you observed about the impact it had on others.

Example

Wrong

Mitch, during the meeting yesterday, you were really rude to Jan when she was explaining her idea. I was appalled.

Better

Mitch, during the meeting yesterday, you kept interrupting Jan when she was explaining her idea. This was making it difficult for her to keep her train of thought as she was talking. After your negative comments, it appeared like she wished she hadn't shared her idea at all. I was really frustrated because I want to encourage everyone on the team to share their ideas for consideration, without worrying about being shut down by others. It looked as though everyone in the room was uncomfortable.

Reaction

Hopefully, Mitch will focus on the behavior as well, and the impact his behavior had on others as objectively as possible. It isn't easy hearing this type of feedback and he may be embarrassed. He may or may not have realized what he was doing. Mitch may have just been trying to help, or he may see Jan as competition and felt threatened by her good idea. He may have wanted to take attention away from her. You won't know unless you address it with him. Make no preconceived assumptions and listen to what Mitch has to say. Try to keep the conversation going as long he needs to talk through it. This will help you learn more about Mitch and his motivation for things that he says and does.

It's important that we all maintain our objectivity when receiving feedback and take care to use neutral or positive words to get the point across. Using negative words when giving this type of feedback makes it more difficult for the receiver to accept.

Positive feedback also needs details. It isn't enough to give vague praise. Let the person know why you are praising him or her.

Wrong

Jan, you did a great job yesterday in the meeting!

Right

Jan, you did a great job summarizing your idea in yesterday's meeting. First, you stated the idea and the impact it would have on the team. Then you outlined the steps need to make it happen. Then you summarized it very succinctly and asked if anyone had questions. It was explained very clearly and a good model for others to follow.

Reaction

Jan really needed to hear this after Mitch disrupted her train of thought during her presentation. There was no "You did a great job but . . ." There was no hidden suggestion. It was just a straight out compliment, containing the details of what Jan did well.

Suppose Jan was not interrupted by Mitch, but could have done some things better when presenting her idea. She jumped into the details before telling the team how it would impact them. It would be appropriate to use the Feedback Sandwich to give her some feedback. The Feedback Sandwich starts and ends with praise, with some constructive feedback sandwiched in the middle.

Example

Jan, I like it that you came up with an idea and were willing to share it with us. It sounds like it has some potential to have a good impact on the team. In order to have the best response and buy-in from the team, it is important to first state the idea and the impact on the team, prior to outlining the details. Without doing that, it left them with a number of additional questions at the end. I think they would have been more receptive as you were going through the details, if they knew where you were going with it. I can help you work through how to do this better for next time. Still, I think they were able to get what you were saying, and I think we should move forward with researching how to make this happen.

This example solidifies that you thought Jan did a good thing by sharing her idea with the team, while making your constructive feedback more palatable.

Body Language as Conversation

BEING A GOOD LEADER requires you to be a good observer. Leaders need to be able to see all the parts and how they fit together. You must always be aware of the "what" and the "why" and whether you are heading toward the goal. When you see clearly what is working well, and what isn't working, you can make necessary adjustments at the right time.

> ▣ *To be a good observer, you must actively observe. This includes paying attention to conversational clues, but also to non-verbal clues.*

During your conversations with others, pay attention to body language. It's a part of the conversation that is often quite telling. Don't make assumptions when you see the folded arms language. If someone has his or her arms folded, it doesn't always mean a lack of openness to what you are saying. It sometimes means the room is cold. If the person is not cold, then they might really be closed to what you are saying. Check the facial expression for further clues.

When a person crosses their arms and rubs their hands against their shoulders, they are either cold or they are pacifying themselves because they feel stressed. A person may also rub their palms down their thighs to pacify themselves when stressed. They also might be wiping sweaty palms because of nervousness.

For an impromptu conversation in the hallway, if the person's body and foot are turned away from you, this person is likely trying to get away and doesn't really want to talk. Even sitting down, check the direction of the body and feet. Is the person hoping to get away quickly? Is the body facing you or away from you? This is telling as to whether they are engaged in the conversation.

Is the person making eye contact? If not, then you don't have their full attention or they are uncomfortable talking to you. Ask yourself why they might be uncomfortable. They might also be shy.

I remember a meeting with one of the IT security people at a company where I once worked, when my team was trying to get permission for some additional access. The security guy across from me at the table seemed tense and was sort of leaning forward when we first started talking. We had been battling a bit in the recent past over this access. As soon as he learned what I wanted on this occasion, and that we could agree on something, he leaned way back in a relaxed pose in the chair, unbuttoned his jacket, and crossed his legs . . . and he smiled. His entire demeanor had suddenly changed. The person on his team who had accompanied him to the meeting suddenly looked really annoyed, as he knew I was getting what I requested (and he had been against it.) The body language said it all.

Aside from all of the things he did—leaning back in the chair, unbuttoning his jacket, and smiling, the person who crosses their legs is showing a sign of being comfortable or confident. If someone changes from having crossed legs to uncrossing them, this indicates that they are becoming more uncomfortable or unhappy. If they have their feet together it indicates they are more submissive, and having their feet apart shows more dominance.

Conducting One-on-Ones

ONE-ON-ONES SHOULD BE a combination of scheduled meetings, **and** also random, informal encounters. Continuous conversations are **continuous** conversations, not **regularly scheduled** conversations.

If you are going to invite someone to have an honest dialogue with you, then you need to be prepared to respond to it appropriately. Don't start defending yourself when someone begins voicing concerns.

Remember the purpose of the conversation—to shake out any obstacles or issues and keep this person engaged and progressing in their work and career. If the person shares an opinion or emotion with you, the conversation emerges into Level 3, which is exactly where you need to be for this conversation to start to have an impact. Don't make the person regret being honest with you. Don't punish them for voicing concerns or try to exert power over them because they questioned a decision you made. The goal was to hear their real concerns, so reinforce them positively and probe with more questions.

Good girl Petunia, keep talking!

Stay focused on the person's reaction and your own reaction to what they are saying, as this is not about winning in a conversation, it's about learning more about the person and how to support them to perform well in a role.

You may be tempted to react in a way that defeats the goal. One part of your brain may cause you to begin to act unconsciously, and you'll need to keep that in check if the conversation gets stressful. There is no competition in a one-on-one.

If the person starts to clam up, or looks angry, and/or backs down to Level 2, then your response may need some work. These are signs that the conversation is not going anywhere and this person is now going through the motions. This is not useful and will have no impact for change or progress.

> ▣ *Confirm your respect for the other person's point of view and clarify the purpose of the discussion or the need for their input, when needed.*

Use your active listening skills consciously and sincerely, as most people are good at detecting insincerity. Respond appropriately to what the person is saying non-verbally, as well as verbally.

Looks of agreement, such as slightly smiling and nodding will encourage the person to continue speaking. Facing the person with your body, rather than facing your body in another direction, tells them you are engaged in the conversation and not waiting for a chance to get away from them.

Active listening is **not** waiting for your turn to speak, but actually taking in what the person is saying. Clarify anything that seems confusing to make sure you understand the message. Use paraphrasing to repeat the message back and ask them to verify this is what they meant. This lets the person know you heard what they said and are making an effort to understand them. Don't look at your watch or doodle or check your phone.

When a person has something on his or her mind, such as an obstacle or issue, it gets in the way of other thinking. It sucks up energy, and distracts from the focus of daily tasks. It can be a relief to discuss it, and get it off one's mind, so that the person can go about the rest of their work without this obstacle or issue hanging over all of their thoughts. This alone is a good reason to have these conversations.

Company culture is created by example. Narratives are formed about the actions that managers take and the engagement and opportunities that people have in their roles. Don't underestimate the importance of each and every conversation you have, and every action that you take as a leader.

At a previous company where I worked, they had a big layoff (following a purchase of the company) about five years before I started working there. For years, I continued to hear stories about the people in the warehouse that were laid off, and how they insisted on staying late that day to make sure all of the shipments went out before they left.

> ⊡ *Company culture has much to do with how engaged people are, and it is built one conversation and one action at a time by leaders.*

Discovery Conversations

IN A ONE-ON-ONE, you may want to have separate conversations about the current role activities vs. development conversations. I suggest having a weekly, bi-weekly, or monthly one-on-one, depending on the person to stay current, aside from your random conversations. A new hire or less autonomous worker may need more frequent meetings. Ensure you are connecting more frequently than bi-weekly or monthly, even if you only meet on that schedule.

During your one-on-one meetings, you can gather information for the development conversations at the same time as you are working on the current conversation. Gather your observed development clues in a separate place from tasks and activities.

There is much to be learned from the tasks and activities conversations that apply to strengths, passions, goals, and possible interests in training or project opportunities. Keep an outline for each person and fill in what you learn after each meeting.

Here are some questions you can ask at a Discovery meeting:

- ☐ What do you want to discuss?

- ☐ What is your biggest obstacle at this moment?

- ☐ What is the most important topic we need to discuss? Describe the issue. What outcome are we looking for? What do you think we need to do to get there? What are the obstacles? What is the impact on you? How do you feel about it?

- ☐ What are the top things that are standing in the way of getting things done? What is the impact on you?

- ☐ What can I do to get things moving forward?

- ☐ What task do you do that you think someone else could do?

- ☐ What do you enjoy most about your role?

- ☐ What do you least enjoy about your role?

- ☐ What feedback/complaints are you hearing about the team?

☐ What's the most important thing the team should do this year? What can you do to impact the team's success?

☐ Do you have any of your own ideas about something we should do?

☐ Do you have any concerns about things we are doing or planning? How do you feel about that?

During one-on-ones, listening and clarifying what is said to you is of the utmost importance. Let the person finish what they are saying. Do not interrupt or assume you know what the issue is, but probe and clarify until you understand the person's point of view.

It's important to learn about each person as an individual and not to depend on one or two people on your team to "fill you in" and give you their perception of everyone and everything that goes on.

⊡ *It's a big mistake to make assumptions based on other people's perceptions, as that perception clouds everything that a person actually says to you. Listen, clarify, question, probe . . .*

Remember, change and development only happen if you converse at Level 3, where emotions and opinions come into play. So it's important during your conversations to ask how the person feels about things or the impact of the issues. If you are just sharing facts, and the person doesn't trust you enough to share an opinion or feeling with you, then you need to work on this relationship in order to connect and engage this person and to inspire growth and development.

When you move past the facts in a conversation, the issues start to emerge. (This is what you want to happen.) The three core issues boil down to these three: Blame, Values, and Choice. What happened? Whose fault was it? Should we or shouldn't we? What are our options?

Determine which issue is at stake and focus on the future outcome, not the past or the present.

☐ What should we do about it?

☐ Why do you think it keeps happening?

☐ What needs to change so that we are better in the future?

⊡ *To help bring emotion into the conversation, ask more questions about the impact of an issue, or how the person feels. Ask what he or she expects to happen if things stay the same, or if a change is implemented.*

Create a form like the one on the following pages to use during your Discovery one-on-ones for your conversations.

Topic List

Issue

Next Steps (Employee)

Next Steps (Me)

Issue

____

____

____

Next Steps (Employee)

____

____

____

Next Steps (Me)

____

____

____

Ideas to Consider

____

____

____

Also create a separate form like the one below to use during your Discovery one-on-ones in preparation for your Development conversations.

Name

____

Strengths

____

____

____

Interests/Possible Goals

____

____

____

Topics of Engagement/Enthusiasm

____

____

____

Possible groups to join

____

____

____

Volunteer Opportunities

____

____

____

Skill Gaps/Challenges

____

____

____

Growth Challenges

____

____

____

Development/Planning Conversations

PREPARATION FOR SETTING development goals begins with the notes you took from your Discovery meetings:

- ☐ What strengths did you identify?

- ☐ What interests/possible goals did you identify?

- ☐ What seems to really engage this person? Have you seen enthusiasm over any particular topic?

- ☐ Possible project or opportunities

- ☐ Group they might join

☐ Volunteer opportunity that might
interest them

☐ Challenges/Skill gaps to overcome

☐ Challenges they might enjoy

⊡ *Ask any questions you think
will get the conversation going,
but remember not to prompt
the person from your list unless
you need it.*

The Discovery list gives you some insight to prompt conversation, but be sure to let the person talk and listen to what they have to say first. It's more effective if you can coax ideas from them. Your notes provide a guideline for this individual to keep things progressing. Use active listening, and ask clarifying questions to ensure that you are understanding their thoughts and words correctly.

Some example questions to ask during a development conversation:

☐ What is the next thing you want to learn
more about?

☐ What educational goals do you have?

☐ What development opportunities or training have you seen that interest you?

☐ Are you involved in any groups inside or outside of the company?

☐ What topics do you find interesting outside of your current role?

☐ How do you feel about training or coaching other people? Are you interested in being in management at some point?

☐ Where are you being sidetracked from being your best self?

☐ With what do people most often ask you to help?

☐ What was your most successful project? What did you enjoy about it? Why?

☐ If you could do something you love every day, what would it be?

☐ What is most likely to cause you to give up on a goal?

☐ What skills do you have that you think are most useful for you?

☐ What skills do you wish you had, and why?

☐ What kind of people do you find interesting?

☐ What are some of your long-term goals?

A strength that is not combined with a person's interest can be a distraction from the intended path. However, sometimes it can open doors to opportunities that serve a purpose and get the person closer to where he or she wants to be.

Agreement Conversations

AT THE END of each one-on-one, review the tasks and agreements from the meeting. Target the outcome that is expected from each item on the list and next steps. Identify which action belongs to which person.

> ▣ *Set up a schedule for progress check-in points, when needed, for specific tasks or a group of tasks. If you have a system that can facilitate tracking and check-ins, this can be a big help.*

Determine metrics, where possible. How often will you be able to track progress using these metrics? Monthly, quarterly?

You can also create a form like the one on the following page to use to facilitate tracking. You may be able to incorporate these headings into a tracking system.

Name

____

Tasks/Goals

____

____

____

Actions Needed & Owner

____

____

____

____

Progress Check-ins

____

____

____

Development Conversations

IF THE EMPLOYEE hasn't always known where his or her passion lies, or has multiple passions, that's okay. He or she will narrow it down eventually. But rather than to be scattered and not very good at any particular thing, have the person pick one or two areas of growth for their focus.

If the person can focus on a few areas to target for growth, he or she will be able to filter through opportunities and recognize the ones that will help him or her move towards goals, rather than to get off track trying everything that comes along.

Setting goals and a direction does not mean that someone has to stay on this path, if they discover that their passion leads in another direction. But if they don't set that path, they will not have a method to filter out distractions that will lead them into a career that looks like a shotgun blast, providing them with a résumé that looks like a scattered target.

Make sure the person understands that it is okay to change a goal, if they find a more suitable one. But urge them to begin by setting some goals and tasks to take them in a direction. It's important to keep moving forward. At some points, it's okay to turn right or left, while steadily moving forward.

As opportunities come along, urge them to think about whether the opportunity will contribute in any subtle or obvious way towards that goal. It can be amazingly easy, once this list is defined.

Once the target growth area or areas have been identified, start identifying the gaps and skills needed to move toward that growth. Then look at training or experience opportunities.

Finally, schedule when and how frequently you will meet to discuss progress. You are already meeting at least once a month to discuss job and role activities, so you can probably meet less often for development. This depends on the nature of the commitments made by the coachee. You will still be adding development notes at your regular one-on-ones. You may have access to a system where progress can be logged and you can correspond more frequently than your face-to-face conversations.

> ▪ *Look for ways to enforce commitment and accountability. If the person is enthusiastic about the plan, the commitment will come easier.*

Follow up to help keep them on track. It really helps if when you have shared a plan of action with someone and they ask you about your progress.

Back when I first started running, I told a friend that I would be running six miles every Sunday. Even when I didn't feel like it, I was afraid she might ask me on Monday if I ran the six miles, and every once in a while she did ask. There were a number of times that I did it just so I wouldn't have to admit that I hadn't.

A guide like the one on the following page can be used for tracking.

Name

____

Growth Areas

____

____

____

Skills Needed

____

____

____

Training Planned

____

____

____

Experiences/Practice

75

____

____

____

Progress Check-ins

____

____

____

Lessons from Stan

STAN EARNS TRUST from the people around him by the way he communicates with them, and by the alignment of his actions. If Stan can do it, then so can you.

Stan remembers key points of earlier conversations to remind people that he heard, understood, and remembered what they said. He uses positive words of encouragement, and elaborates on details when he is praising someone. When sharing constructive feedback, it is brief and to the point. He focuses on the situation and behavior, and uses the feedback sandwich when appropriate.

He reacts by listening and not interrupting, when someone voices concerns. Stan uses paraphrasing and asks questions to ensure he understands the intent of what he hears. He shows his enthusiasm for other people's accomplishments, and shows that he cares in many different ways. He doesn't judge an individual's words by what someone else told him.

Stan's sincerity shows through in his conversations both verbally and non-verbally. He makes himself available to listen and guide others, even outside of their scheduled meetings. He lets people know he will make time for them, so they won't be reluctant to ask. He has worked hard to become a servant leader, and is sincerely committed toward the growth of each and every person in his life to succeed. His team works well together and meets all of their goals.

With your heart and mind both engaged, you, too, can be a successful leader like Stan.

Other Books by Emily Nightingale

IF YOU ENJOYED this book, please check Amazon for other books by Emily Nightingale.

The Successful Millennial:
Tips for Navigating the Corporate Jungle
More than 100 tips are provided to help you navigate more proficiently in the corporate workplace with colleagues and leaders, and become recognized for your expertise and style.

Become a Big Picture Thinker:
Learn How to Think Big
In this book, you'll learn more about the advantages of Big Picture Thinking for planning, problem

solving, inventing new products, or improving the world around you. You'll also discover how to identify your own thinking type, and the steps you can take to become more proficient in the completion and implementation of your ideas.

Get Promoted:
Two Strategies That Work
Learn about the two most important strategies to help you get promoted.

Review Request

THANK YOU FOR taking the time to read this book. I hope you enjoyed it and found the information to be useful.

I would love to have your feedback, and would be grateful if you would post an honest review of the book. I love learning more about the reader's point of view. Your support and feedback does make a difference.

To leave a review, please visit *Coaching Conversations that Count—Leading Teams with Continuous Conversations* book page on Amazon.com. Scroll down to the Customer Reviews section. Locate the button labeled "Write a customer review" and click the button to enter your review.

Thank you in advance for your feedback!

Bibliography

"Active Listening." *SkillsYouNeed*, www.skill-syouneed.com/ips/active-listening.html.

"Do You Know the 4 Levels of Conversation?" *Balancing Change Mindfully*, 28 Aug. Gilkey, Charlie, et al. "The Four Levels of Communication." *Productive Flourishing*, 29 Aug. 2019, www.productiveflourishing.com/four-levels-of-communication/.

Glaser, Judith E. *Conversational Intelligence: How Great Leaders Build Trust and Get Extraordinary Results*. Routledge, 2016.

Greenleaf, Robert. "Ten Principles." *Servant Leader Journal*, The Capacity Building Institute, www.servantleaderjournal.com/ten-principles.html.

Heinrichs, Jay. *Thank You for Arguing: What Aristotle, Lincoln, and Homer Simpson Can Teach Us about the Art of Persuasion*. Three Rivers Press, 2017.

Jasper, Rebecca. "Do You Know the 4 Levels of Conversation?" *Balancing Change Mindfully*, 23 July 2014, balancingchangemindfully.com/do-you-know-the-4-levels-of-conversation/.

Navarro, Joe, and Marvin Karlins. *What Every BODY Is Saying: an Ex-FBI Agent's Guide to Speed-Reading People*. Harper Collins, 2015.

Patterson, Kerry, et al. *Crucial Conversations: Tools for Talking When Stakes Are High*. McGraw-Hill, 2012.

Rath, Tom. *Strengthsfinder 2.0*. Gallup Press, 2017.

Scott, Kim. *Radical Candor: Be a Kick-Ass Boss without Losing Your Humanity*. St Martin's Press, 2019.

Scott, Susan. *Fierce Conversations: Achieving Success at Work & in Life, One Conversation at a Time*. Berkley, 2017.

Stanier, Michael Bungay. *The Coaching Habit Say Less, Ask More & Change the Way You Lead Forever*. Box of Crayons Press, 2016.